# Making Dickie Happy

## by
## Jeremy Kingston

**Published by Playdead Press 2013**

© Jeremy Kingston

Jeremy Kingston has asserted his rights under the Copyright, Design and Patents Act, 1988, to be identified as the author of this work.

A CIP catalogue record for this book is available from the British Library.

ISBN 978-0-9575266-7-9

**Playdead Press**
**www.playdeadpress.com**

*Making Dickie Happy* premiered at the Rosemary Branch
Theatre on 13th September 2004. The cast was as follows:

**Noel Coward**          Robert Forknall

**Dickie Mountbatten**   Hywel John

**Agatha Christie**      Caroline Wildi

**Tono**                 David Peto

**J-Boy**                Matt Reeves

**Cyril**                Rob Pomfret


*Directed by* Robert Gillespie

*Designed by* Kevin Freeman

*Lighting by* Stephen Ley

*Stage Manager* Hugh Allison

*Making Dickie Happy* was revived at the Tristan Bates Theatre, with its first performance taking place on 5th March 2013. The cast was as follows:

| | |
|---|---|
| **Noel Coward** | Phineas Pett |
| **Dickie Mountbatten** | James Phelips |
| **Agatha Christie** | Helen Duff |
| **Tono** | David Alderman |
| **J-Boy** | Matthew Alexander |
| **Cyril** | Rob Pomfret |

*Directed by* Robert Gillespie

*Designed by* Gregor Donnelly

*Lighting by* Rob Mills

*Stage Manager* Fana Cioban

*Casting by* Clare Cameron

*Production Consultant* John Nicholls, Arts Quarter

*Media Relations* Target Live

## Author's Note

The idea for this play took its first vague shape when I discovered that Coward, Mountbatten and Agatha Christie all used to visit the same hotel, on Burgh Island off the south coast of Devon. I wondered if an encounter between these three might be worth exploring, especially if it could take place while they were still only at the threshold of their careers. The result might resemble a Christie detective story with, hopefully, some of the wit of a Coward comedy.

But if it was to be a Christie then what was the crime? At this point I unearthed the astonishing fact that it was Mountbatten who suggested to Agatha Christie the 'treacherous' plot she eventually used in her innovative novel *The Murder of Roger Ackroyd*. I would never have dared to invent such an incredible event, and it provided the focus and dramatic line for the ideas on life and love and partnership that I realised I wanted to express in this play.

The song 'Devon' comes from Noël Coward's first revue *London Calling!* though he was only Noel Coward back then. The lyrics seem to have appeared in print only in a 1931 collection of his revue material and the music appears not to have been published at all. Coward rewrote the song in the 1950s for his cabaret season at the Café de Paris but the original score was only recovered with the aid of Peter Greenwell, Coward's last accompanist. He delved into his archives and came up with a 1923 piano selection of music from *London Calling!* that included a passage recognisably from 'Devon'. Its performance in this play is probably the first time it has been publicly sung since then.

**Jeremy Kingston**

## Director's Note

Besides all the elegant interplay between life and art which the play contains – I was most encouraged to find the sound thesis that all attempts at relationships between humans (of whatever sexual persuasion) must end in compromise; as all the couplings of this play do; and are no worse for that, given that nothing much else is possible – except in books.

**Robert Gillespie**

## The Playwright

### Jeremy Kingston (Playwright)

Jeremy Kingston was born in London and brought up in various Home Counties before returning to live in London. Two of his stage plays have been produced in the West End and more on the Fringe, most recently *Oedipus at the Crossroads* and *Making Dickie Happy*. He is the author of a novel *Love Among the Unicorns* and two children's books. For ten years he was the theatre critic of *Punch* and for the past twenty has been a theatre critic on *The Times*. His first poetry collection *On the Lookout* appeared in 2008.

## Cast

### Phineas Pett (Noel Coward)

Phineas trained at the Drama Centre and the Vakhtangov Institue in Moscow after reading Modern Languages at Exeter University.

Theatre includes- *The Importance of Being Earnest* (Tour), *The Proposal* (MOMA NY/SF), *The God of Soho* (Shakespeare's Globe), *Romeo and Juliet* (Tour), *Zaide* (Tour),*1888* (Union Theatre), *Cymbeline* (RSC Studio), *Seven Other Children* (New End/Bolton Octagon), *A Yorkshire Tragedy* (White Bear) *Olive Juice* (NT Studio), *The Diary* (Riverside Studios).

Television includes: *Mexico City, The Interrogators, Buck Diablo is Dead* and *Inspector Boyle Investigates*.

Phineas was also in the first cast of the *24 Hour Plays* at the Old Vic.

### James Phelips (Dickie)

James trained at RADA and has recently played the title
role in Shakespeare's *Pericles* at the Rose Theatre Studio,
Kingston.

Before training at RADA, James took part in many
National Youth Theatre productions, including *Savages* at
The Royal Court Theatre, directed by Edward Kemp,
*Henry V* at the Hackney Empire, directed by Paul Roseby,
*Cell Sell* directed by Stella Duffy at the Soho Theatre and
*Lorca in a Green Dress*, directed by Andrew Steggall at the
Arcola Theatre.

Credits while training included: *Our Town* directed by
Geraldine Alexander, *A Waste of Time* directed by Jane
Bertish and *Pornography* directed by Trilby James.

### Helen Duff (Agatha Christie)

Helen graduated from LAMDA after studying English
Literature at Cambridge University.

Credits include: *Dead Pile* (Nance, Old Vic TS Eliot
Exchange) *Happy New (* Pru, Old Red Lion), *The Sexual
Awakening of Peter Mayo* (Thursday Afternoon, Pleasance
Courtyard / Theatre 503) and in The Old Vic's 24 Hour
Plays and Time Warner Ignite Project. Credits while
training include: *Hedda Gabler* (Hedda Gabler,
Joseph Blatchley), *The Talented Mr
Ripley* (Emily Greenleaf / Aunt Dottie, James Kerr), *Daisy
Pulls It Off* (Monica Smithers, Stephen
Jameson), *Touched* (Bridie, Colin Cook) and *Twelfth
Night* (Viola, Lucy Kerbel). Parts played at Cambridge

include: *Titus Andronicus* (Tamora, Action To The Word), *Macbeth* (Lady Macbeth, European Theatre Group Tour) and *Greek* (Mum/Sphinx, Alexandra Spencer Jones).

## David Alderman (Tono)

David Alderman trained at Drama Studio London.

Theatre includes*: Once Seen* (Battersea Mess & Music Hall), *Lady Windermere's Fan, Look Back in Anger* (European Tour), *Pool (no water)* (Norwich Playhouse), *Army of Reason* (Edinburgh Festival, Pleasance), *Caligula* (Union Theatre), *Romeo & Juliet* (French Tour), *Twelfth Night* (Theatre Royal Margate).

TV includes: *Casualty, Crimewatch*, various BBC promos, and numerous commercials including the current 'Nationwide Building Society' campaign.
Film includes: *Callback Queen, Take 3 Girls, Ghosts of Guantanamo.*

## Matthew Alexander (J-Boy)

Matthew trained at the Royal Central School of Speech and Drama. He graduated in 2011.

Professional credits include: *Holby City* (BBC) and *As You Like It* (Custom/Practice)
Credits whilst training include: King Lear / *King Lear*, Eddie Carbone / *A View From The Bridge*, Jaques / *As You Like It* and Orestes / *The Orestia*.

**Rob Pomfret (Cyril)**

Rob turned his back on the medical profession to pursue a career in acting. He has interspersed performing in critically acclaimed productions on the London and Edinburgh stage with sojourns in the Far East and South America. Through popular demand he is reprieving the role of Cyril for the first time since its inaugural run.

Rob first worked with Robert Gillespie in Jeremy's *Oedipus at the Crossroads* and has enjoyed a productive relationship since playing many character roles including gaining Critics' Choice for his performance of the Dromio twins in *Comedy of Errors*.

## Creative

### Robert Gillespie, Director

Robert Gillespie is mainly associated with new writing as a director and is the founder of Jane Nightwork Productions, a company dedicated to performing texts neglected by both commercial and 'avant-garde' theatre . He has contributed to seventeen productions at the King's Head Theatre, most of them world premieres. He has directed a number of Jeremy's plays including the first acclaimed production of *Making Dickie Happy* (Rosemary Branch Theatre), *Oedipus at the Crossroads* (King's Head). He has contributed shows to six Dublin Theatre Festivals and worked in Israel on, amongst other plays, Frayn's *Noises Off* (1980) at the Cameri Theatre, Tel Aviv.

Robert is probably best known as a TV sit-com actor, and starred as Dudley Rush, a part written for him by Brian Cooke, in five series of *Keep it in the Family* for Thames Television. Other credits include *Likely Lads, Dad's Army, Rising Damp and Porridge*. Recently, he featured in Cardboard Citizens' striking production of their WWII epic – *Mincemeat*.

To keep up to speed with the work of Jane Nightwork productions, please go to www.janenightwork.com or follow the company on Twitter @JaneNightwork

### Gregor Donnelly, Set and Costume Designer

Gregor was born in Edinburgh and trained in Set and Costume Design on the Motley Theatre Design Course, London.

Designs include: *The Mikado, Trial by Jury* and *The Zoo (Rosemary Branch Theatre) La Bohème (*Thaxted Theatre) *A Dinner Engagement* and *Comedy on the Bridge (*King's Head Theatre) *Susanna's Secret (*King's Head Theatre) *La Bohème* (revival design for OperaUpClose) *Barber of Seville* (OperaUpClose tour) *Night Music* (Guildhall School of Music and Drama).

*The Hot Mikado and Oliver!* (Churchill Theatre, Edinburgh) *Jekyll & Hyde* (St Brides Centre) *The Rink* (Edinburgh Festival) *Honk* (Boroughmuir Theatre) the Ivor Novello musical *Perchance to Dream* (Finborough Theatre) *The Devil Always Gets The Best Tunes* (Drill Hall) *Acorn Antiques* (Churchill Theatre, Edinburgh, Associate Designer) *The World Goes Round* (Canal Cafe Theatre) *Gay's the Word* (Jermyn Street Theatre), *Someone to Blame* (King's Head Theatre).

Costume Designer on Arthur Miller's *The American Clock,* Sutton Vane's *Outward Bound* and the sell-out production of *Drama at Inish* directed by Fidelis Morgan starring Celia Imrie and Paul O'Grady all for the Finborough Theatre. *DirtyDating.Com* (Stockport Plaza and Epstein Theatre, Liverpool)

Current designs include *Daisy Pulls it Off* (Gatehouse Theatre) which is running from March 8th-l 14th April 2013, and *Les Misérables* (ESMS Edinburgh).

### Rob Mills, Lighting Designer

Working principally in theatre and opera, Rob's work also covers corporate and live events.

Recents Credits as Lighting Designer include: *Gay's the Word* (Jermyn St & Finborough), *Tosca* (UK Touring & Luxembourg National Cultural Centre), *Napoleon Noir* (Shaw Theatre), *Gilbert is Dead* (Hoxton Hall), *Romeo & Juliet* (Cambridge Arts Theatre), *Love Bites* (Leatherhead Theatre), *Curtains* (Landor), *The Elixir of Love* (Stanley Hall Opera), *The Lion the Witch and the Wardrobe* and *Hayton on Homicide* (Edinburgh), *Niceties* (Cambridge Footlights).

As Production & Lighting Designer work includes: *Aida* (Epsom Playhouse), *Madama Butterfly* (Harlequin Theatre), *Venus & Adonis, Dido & Aeneas* and *The Magic Flute* (Upstairs at the Gatehouse), *The Mikado and Yeomen of the Guard* (Minack Theatre), *The Mikado* (Cambridge Arts Theatre), *Don Giovanni & Pelléas et Mélisande* (West Rd Concert Hall, *Crave* (Edinburgh). Rob has also provided the lighting & event design for a number of live and corporate events, including the 2010 'Floating Finale' to the Lord Mayor's Show, on the River Thames. He is the founder of bespoke event design company Light Motif.

For more information see: www.robwmills.co.uk

**Fana Cioban, Stage Manager**

Fana is a Romanian director and stage manager based in London. She studied in Romania, London (East 15 Acting School, 2011), Bali and Moscow.

Recent stage management credits are: *Mass-Observation by Inspector Sands* (Newbury Corn Exchange, Newbury; Almeida, London, July 2012*); A Beginning, a middle and* *an end/ What the animals say by Greyscale* (Traverse, Edinburgh; Northern Stage, Newcastle; Hull Truck, Hull; Tron, Glasgow and CPT, Camden, Autumn 2012) and *The Ballad of Mick//scratch by Penny Dreadful* (The Lowry, Manchester, January 2013). Recent directing and assisting directing credits: *Otto* (GalataPerform, Istanbul); *Theatre Uncut* (Young Vic); *Gabrielle's Kitchen* (Lost Theatre); *Denial* (King's Head Theatre); *The Ninth Plague* (Unicorn Theatre, London).

## Clare Cameron, Casting

Clare is an actress and Associate Director of Jane Nightwork Productions. As an actress work includes, for stage: Jenny Young in *Denial* (King's Head Theatre), Phoebe Henville in *Someone to Blame* (King's Head Theatre), Marie-Sidonie Cressaux in *Queens of France* (Leatherhead Theatre), Maria in *Love, Question Mark* (Jane Nightwork Productions), The Architect in *Like A Fishbone* (The Cockpit), Corinne in *The Country* (Mountview), Caliban in *The Tempest* (The Cock Tavern), *You've Been A Wonderful Audience* (Baron's Court Theatre), *Macbeth* and *The Taming of the Shrew* (Cambridge Shakespeare Festival), Jane Austen in *Jane Austen Makes a Match* (UK Tour), Christina Rossetti in *Loving Ophelia* (Pleasance London), Nell Gwynne in *Playhouse Creatures* (The Chapterhouse Theatre). Rehearsed readings: *Useless Mouths* (National Theatre Studio/Jane Nightwork Productions), *Chains* (Trafalgar Studios), *How to be a Good Zimbabwean* (Oval House Theatre), *All Our Yesterdays* (Blue Elephant Theatre). TV and film includes Mary Boleyn in *Henry VIII* (ITV), *The Turing Enigma, Cab Hustle* and *Beneath Our Masks*.

Reviews, interviews and more can be found at
www.clarecameron.com or follow Clare on Twitter
@1ClareCameron

**John Nicholls at Arts Quarter, Production Consultant**

John founded Arts Quarter in 2008. He has some 25 years'
experience of working within the arts, wider charitable
communities and creative industries in the UK and
overseas. At AQ, he has overall responsibility for the
strategic direction of the partnership in addition to
managing the firm's research programmes. John also works
with a wide range of clients across all areas of the firm's
core business areas as well as developing its learning and
professional development programmes.

In addition to serving as Managing Partner of AQ, John is
a Governor of Trinity Laban Conservatoire of Music &
Dance and a Trustee of South East Dance, where he is also
Chair of the Development Committee. In the past, he has
served as a Trustee of National AIDS Trust, Headlong
Theatre and Campaign for Drawing and was Chair of
Pacitti Company. He also acts as ad-hoc advisor to a range
of other arts organisations at Board level. John has worked
with Jane Nightwork Productions since 2011.
For more information visit www.artsquarter.co.uk or
follow John and the team on Twitter @ArtsQuarter

**The Tristan Bates Theatre** is a 70-seat studio theatre in central London, the Tristan Bates Theatre has a reputation for supporting and showcasing new writing, contemporary productions and work by regional and international companies. The venue offers an ideal destination for audiences in the heart of the West End and Covent Garden, alongside having strong industry connections through the Actors Centre.

The Tristan Bates Theatre as part of the Actors Centre has a vision to support actors, artists and companies not just to achieve the best possible work, but to develop on to the next stages of their careers. Programme highlights in 2012 included the acclaimed European premiere of musical *The Last Session* starring Darren Day; Nirjay Mahindru's *Golgotha* directed by Iqbal Khan (*Broken Glass*, Tricycle/West End; RSC's *Much Ado*); and *DYSPLA*, the UK's Festival of work by dyslexic storymakers. The building's patrons are David Harewood MBE, Joely Richardson and Rafe Spall.

**www.tristanbatestheatre.co.uk**

The *Making Dickie Happy* team would like to thank Stephen Waley-Cohen, Edward Kemp, Ben Monks, Will Young, the Actors Centre, Paul Warrington and TCE Creative

With special thanks to John Nicholls, Greg Jameson, Elliot Robinson and Hanna Pianos of Wimbledon.

*Making Dickie Happy* has been made possible by
generous sponsorship from Hanna Pianos

**CAST**

CYRIL

LORD  BUNGAY  (Tono)

AGATHA CHRISTIE

NOEL COWARD

LIEUT. JAMES INCHPEN (J-Boy)

LIEUT. LORD LOUIS MOUNTBATTEN (Dickie)

ACT ONE

Scene 1

*A public room in a hotel on a small island off the coast of Devon. The early 1920s. Summer. Morning. White chairs placed around low white tables. A white grand piano. Three arches: R to the hotel foyer and bar; C up a couple of steps to a corridor; L to a sun lounge.*

*LORD BUNGAY (TONO), early 20s, is seated, leafing through a* Strand Magazine. *CYRIL, a barman, early 20s, enters with a cocktail, places it on TONO's table. TONO rests a hand upon Cyril's.*

CYRIL            My lord?

*TONO moues a kiss. CYRIL glances around, kisses him.*

                 Will there be anything else, my lord?

*TONO expressionless.*

                 Thank you, my lord.

*CYRIL exits.*
*TONO drinks his cocktail, stands, stares out front.*

TONO            Fuck.

*Takes cigarette from case, feels for lighter.*

2

Double fuck.

*Glances at tables for matches, exits after CYRIL. AGATHA CHRISTIE enters C. In her early 30s, auburn-haired, married and the mother of a small daughter. At this early stage in her career she has written a couple of Hercule Poirot novels and a volume of Poirot stories. She can be unpredictably nervous with strangers. After a moment she sits at the piano. After a moment she lifts the keyboard lid. After a moment TONO returns, smoking his cigarette, waits in the archway. After a moment AGATHA turns and sees him.*

TONO            I didn't wish to disturb you.

AGATHA          Not at all. I was only thinking of playing, not intending to play.   The tone isn't good.

TONO            The salt air, perhaps.

AGATHA          Though it would be, if looked after. There used to be a Broadwood here before the War.   Not so glamorous, but it knew it was meant to be a piano and not a cocktail cabinet.

TONO            May I order you a cocktail?

AGATHA          No, thank you. Lord Bungay, I think?

TONO            Good morning.

*Pause*

                    Before the War?

AGATHA              Yes.

TONO                But all this is very modern.

AGATHA              Oh, yes.

TONO                Mrs Jennings, too, she's very modern.

AGATHA              Young Mrs Jennings.

TONO                And old Mrs Jennings?

AGATHA              The old hotel burned down.

TONO                Ah. And the old Broadwood.

AGATHA              I suppose so. What a great pity. But the
view of the sea and the cliffs and the air is the same. It's
no use moaning about it and groaning about it and going
on and on about how things aren't what they were and
aren't what they could be and aren't what — *(breaks off)*

*Pause*

TONO                Why not?

4

AGATHA          Well, well, one wouldn't get anywhere. Well, one would get, yes, one would get somewhere but would one want — to be there? A clean sweep and start again has always been my — my — I've tried to make that my — *(finally breaks off)*

TONO            The only sweep I've met was conspicuously sooty.

AGATHA          Yes, that's very clever.

*TONO picks up his magazine.*

                You have the latest *Strand Magazine*?

TONO            Bought in the Strand yesterday.

AGATHA          Last month they published Part One of the new Sherlock Holmes story. 'Thor Bridge'. Quite the best thing he's written for I don't know how many years.

TONO            *(offers magazine to her)*  Part Two.

AGATHA          But have you finished with it?

TONO            Practically. That's to say, I've finished it. I just haven't begun it. Mr Coward is twitching to talk about it but honour bound not to until I have found out how the deed was done.

AGATHA          The wife killed herself, presumably, and made it look like murder.

TONO          Do you wish me to tell you?

AGATHA          It couldn't be anything else.

TONO          Even though her body is lying on the bridge, shot through the head and no gun in her hand?

AGATHA          Oh, yes, I daresay.

TONO          What about the husband's mistress? Five minutes earlier they were seen quarrelling on the bridge.

AGATHA          But everyone calls her a saint. The husband denies she's his mistress. Of course. Naturally. Which Sherlock Holmes believes.

TONO          *(reads)* 'I can never forget the effect which Miss Dunbar produced upon me. That strong, clear-cut, yet sensitive face — '

AGATHA          Dr Watson, no doubt. Pole-axed again by the female sex. So she'll be innocent.

*She holds out her hand for the magazine. TONO gives it to her.*

The only clue is a chip on the underside of the parapet of the bridge. So presumably Mrs . . . Gibson tied a length of string to a gun. She fastened the other end to something heavy and dangled that over the parapet. When she shot herself the gun would have flown out of her hand — *(reads)* ' — sharp crack against the parapet and vanished over the side into the water.' Precisely.

TONO          I'm most impressed by your deduction, Mrs — ?

AGATHA          Clifford. Room 6.

TONO          Perhaps you should be a detective.

AGATHA          *(returns the magazine)* Scotland Yard once asked Conan Doyle to assist them on a case. He was no help at all.

*TONO has taken out another cigarette. Still without the means to light it, he returns the cigarette to his case.*

          Please do. My husband smokes like a mill chimney.

*TONO rings the bell.*

TONO          It is a splendid view.

*AGATHA sits at the piano and launches into something turbulent, perhaps Schumann's Kreisleriana, No 7.*
*CYRIL enters.*
*TONO indicates his unlit cigarette. CYRIL lights it.*
*AGATHA stops playing.*

Please go on. Isn't it Brahms?

AGATHA          That's all I needed to play. The flowers in the dining-room are not being watered.

CYRIL          I'm sorry, ma'am.

AGATHA          I'm sure there are plenty more where they came from but that's not the point, is it? They have days of life left in them yet so why let them keel over?

CYRIL          I'll see to it at once, ma'am.

AGATHA          Thank you. It's probably not your responsibility. Mrs Jennings ought to see to it.

CYRIL          I'll speak to her, ma'am.

AGATHA          Because they're very handsome. And well-arranged too. Don't you think?

TONO          I hadn't, I must admit, noticed them.

AGATHA     Oh, they are. Well chosen. Bold reds against the yellow.

TONO     Splashes of blood.

AGATHA     Well, no.  Well, yes, if you want to be fanciful.

TONO     Thank you, Cyril.

CYRIL     Thank you, my lord.

AGATHA     You won't forget?

CYRIL     No, ma'am.

*CYRIL exits.*

AGATHA     Perhaps I've done my share of meddling for the day. But I was brought up not to countenance waste, or recklessness of any kind.  Well, I — *(she prepares to leave)* I believe I was  introduced to your mother. Before the War in Cairo.

TONO     She was with her husband? My father?

AGATHA     He was a striking man. I found him courteous and, in his way, encouraging.

TONO            I've heard people say there is that side
to him. You are fortunate to have noticed it.

*NOEL COWARD enters, with CYRIL. In his early 20s, two
of his plays have been produced in London with modest
success. A hit revue has made him a minor celebrity but real
success lies ahead.*

NOEL            Tono, did you know that Cyril's father
was in the profession?

TONO            Which profession?

CYRIL           Not a performer, my lord.

NOEL            Stuff and nonsense. How do you do?
Who isn't a performer   in   the   theatre?   The   seller   of
programmes, the shifter of scenes, the old stager at the
door. They perform better than many   actresses   I   could
name who imagine the way to create a character is to treat
the   author's   script   like   a   sort   of   literary   North   West
Passage.  Nobody feels any confidence in it but they might
as well set sail in its general direction. You seem   alarmed.

CYRIL           No, sir.

NOEL            *(to TONO)* Don't you feel that?

TONO            Feel what?

NOEL            To be sure.  You may be fatigued?

CYRIL           No, sir.

NOEL            What it is to have youth on one's side.
Though some prefer to have their youth on top of them.
Bring us two more of your green-eyed goddesses.

CYRIL           Very good, sir.

NOEL            A cocktail?

AGATHA          *(mouths)* No, thank you.

NOEL            How wise. Cyril refuses to say how
many sticky liquors go into his shaker.

*CYRIL exits.*

                Ambrosia, nectar, a dash of spleen.
Have you managed to crawl your way to the end of 'Thor
Bridge'?

TONO            The wife killed herself.

NOEL            A simple Yes or No would have
sufficed. I'm sorry to say Lord Bungay comes from a
family of blabbermouths. Do you wish me to give him a
clip round the lug-hole?

TONO          She wanted to make people think the
husband's mistress killed her.

NOEL          The story contains a message for us all.
— Don't frown. Lift an eyebrow, never frown. — He is
writing about himself.

TONO          Conan Doyle's wife shot herself on a
bridge?

NOEL          Try a mite harder.

TONO          He shot her on a bridge.

NOEL          The first Lady Doyle died from
carefully extended ill-health thirteen years after Sir Arthur
fell in love with a younger woman. For thirteen years he
mewed and moped but didn't dare make her his mistress.
He doesn't know he is writing about himself. Keeping
personal history out of one's writing requires constant
vigilance, Mrs — ?

TONO          Clifford.

NOEL          Blink and the little clues pop out, hop,
skip and a jump. Sir Arthur blinked and blinked and out
they pour, like bats from a sinking belfry. The wife he has
outgrown but refused to abandon. The impatience for her
death that turned to hatred. The abuse that Mrs —

TONO          Clifford.

*A beat.*

NOEL          . . . Gibson hurls against her husband's mistress is the abuse he has hurled against himself. Here it is, for all the world to read, the unspoken wish that his wife should have killed herself thirteen years ago, before his brain turned into a doughnut. Because she didn't, he has all but killed his genius, and this is its swansong.

AGATHA       Lady Doyle may not have grasped the fact that she ought to kill herself to make her husband happy.

NOEL          His crime was to go on living with her.

AGATHA       A crime for a man to live with his wife?

NOEL          The crime was committed against himself. Once he was a man of action, as you can tell from his bulging adverbs. For thirteen years he has written rubbish because he has turned himself into rubbish. Better one last song than silence. But how much better a song cycle year after year. 'Thor Bridge'. 'Wotan Bridge'. 'Brünnhilde Bridge' . . .

TONO          What is this message for us all?

NOEL          Watch your tongue.

13

*A distant gunshot. They turn their heads.*

I shall write a detective story myself and set it on this island. At high tide Mrs Brainwaring was alive and pruning the montbretias. Before the ferry arrived her body was found with an Andalusian rapier sticking out of her midriff. 'No one 'as left ze island,' says the funny little detective who 'as come there to study ze amorous 'abits of ze puffin. Or ze guillemot. Or ze penguin.

AGATHA          I doubt that anyone would find penguins where there are montbretias.

*During the next speech CYRIL enters with cocktails.*

NOEL          It is the vital clue. To bring the montbretias into flower their rhizomes were sprayed with a Patagonian fertilizer to which Mrs Brainwaring was allergic. The only person to know this was Tono, are you flirting with a hired hand?

TONO          Naturally.

NOEL          I doubt that. Thank you, Cyril.

CYRIL          Thank you, sir. My lord.

*CYRIL exits.*

NOEL            We should never have come to this
rock.  I understand why Napoleon died on St Helena.

TONO            You exaggerate.

NOEL            The enterprise had disaster written all
over it.

TONO            You should have taken the trouble to
say so.

NOEL            How possibly, with you determined to
come here and pick up seaweed?

*TONO comes to NOEL for a light for his cigarette.*

                Having traded your cigarette lighter for
crabs.

TONO            Please.

AGATHA          I must away.  Mr Coward, I cannot
pretend I care for your views on marriage.

NOEL            They are my honest views, Mrs Clifford.
Mrs Arabelle Clifford?  I know it's bad form to read an
hotel register but I never resist the chance to look at a little
light fiction.  I generally sign myself Nicolas Copernicus.
On special occasions, Natasha Chekhov.

AGATHA          Good morning.

*She exits.*

NOEL          Arabelle Clifford, how perfectly fatuous.
She has gone plodding off to see how long it would take a
murderer to carry a corpse from here to the smugglers' cove
on the other side.  And if you cannot keep that glint from
your eye she will make the murderer you.

TONO          Are you certain she's who you think she
is?

NOEL          Not the iota of a doubt.  What game do
you suppose she's  playing?

TONO          Tracking somebody?

NOEL          Who knows her name but not her face?
I knew her name and face.  When the *Sketch* serialized her
stories it spattered the pages with photographic studies of
the authoress at home.   With her daughter: the smile
indulgent.  With pipe-smoking husband: the smile dutiful.
With her trusty Corona: ears pricked to catch the pipings
of her muse.  Tracking who?

TONO          The husband's mistress.

NOEL          Too obvious.  Twice I gave her her cue
to crumple at the knees and cry, 'It's a fair cop, guv!'  She

16

knows she is rumbled but will not climb down from her rumble.

TONO           She's in hiding.

NOEL           Better.

TONO           From Mr Christie, who is a Bolshevik spy.

NOEL           She plays with her wedding ring.

TONO           She wants to leave him.  No.

NOEL           He wants to leave her.

TONO           Then why is she hiding?  He wants to murder her.

NOEL           She wants to murder him.

TONO           Then why is she hiding?

NOEL           So she can't murder him.  These are deep waters and we have imprudently come without our bathing costumes.

TONO           *(with a glance down R)* Someone has come off the boat.

NOEL            Spare me. Mother. Queen Mary.

TONO            Getting warm.

NOEL            Dear Ivor.

TONO            Why would Ivor come here?

NOEL            Ned was telling everyone within screeching distance of the prowess of some chunky Ganymede. Cyril or his mate.

TONO            He was talking of Gerard at the Metropole.

NOEL            The nigger boxer with the vaselined eyelids? Hardly Ivor's tumbler of punch.

TONO            Ivor wasn't there. Why are we talking of him? Gerard? Ned? I sometimes think you only talk to fill up the air.

NOEL            I don't believe I can ever forgive you that remark. Certainly I shall make no effort to forget. Fill up the air. I do forgive you. And I've forgotten. But you do see why we should have gone somewhere else. In Paris I could have typed my fingers to the bone while you dangled your feet in the Seine. You look so comely, with the light just catching the tilt of your nose. Filling up the air.

*TONO comes over to him, pats his shoulder.*

                Come, come.  None of that.

TONO            We can leave, if you like.  Now.  Yes,
let's go.

NOEL              No, no.

TONO            I'd like us to.

NOEL              Cyril would be disappointed.

                *TONO stares at him.*

                I'm sorry.  I'm sorry.

                *He holds out an arm.  They hold arms.*

                Why am I not at ease?

TONO            We could be in Paris this time
tomorrow.

*CYRIL enters and sets bowls of nuts on the tables.*

                We'll stay at the Valois again. Sit at the
window table at the Gropinard.

NOEL                    You are an unreformed sentimentalist.
It's perfectly engaging.

CYRIL                   I must apologize, sir, for the condition
of the nuts.  They are definitely below par.

NOEL                    Send them my condolences and some
fruit.

CYRIL                   It's the sea air, sir.  The salt effloresces
and makes a mockery of our endeavours.

NOEL                    This pistachio is delicious.

CYRIL                   It's good of you to say so, sir, but in my
heart of hearts I know you only do it to be kind.

*CYRIL departs.  TONO and NOEL double up with laughter.*

TONO                    No.  No, he's a bunny.

NOEL                    And so are you.  And so am I.  And what
friends are about to join the warren?

*LIEUTENANT JAMES (J-BOY) INCHPEN appears
in archway R.  Early 20s.*

TONO                    J-boy!

J-BOY             Tono! Noel! Good God. Dickie, we're too late.

*LIEUTENANT LORD LOUIS (DICKIE)*
*MOUNTBATTEN joins him. In his early 20s, his practised*
*charm conceals insecurity, in part caused by his position at the*
*fringe of several royal families.*

            How long have you been here, you rogue?

TONO             Yesterday.

J-BOY             Why this hole?

DICKIE             Noel! How amazing!

TONO             Why you?

NOEL             Dickie.

J-BOY             Why not! And beaten to it.

DICKIE             Noel's here.

NOEL             Beaten to what? Tono? Too late? You're up to something.

TONO             *(calling)* Cyril!

NOEL            Shouldn't you be on your boat?

DICKIE          Ship.  No.

J-BOY           Yes.

TONO            We can play that game Eddie showed
us.  One of us says a word and the next one says the first
word to come into his head.

DICKIE          Why?

TONO            Valley.

DICKIE          What?

TONO            Tyler.

NOEL            Do stop that nonsense, Tono.  It's divine
to see you, Dickie.  And you, J-Boy.  Was machst du hier?

DICKIE          Weiss nicht.

J-BOY           Sight-seeing.  Bobby Anstruther  says
there is something spectacular on the premises.

NOEL            Who can he have meant?

TONO            Dennis is visiting his Mum in Exeter
but Cyril is on show.

*CYRIL enters.*

NOEL          Talk of the angel.

CYRIL         My lord?

*TONO glances at DICKIE and J-BOY.*

DICKIE       Whisky and soda.  No soda.

J-BOY         The same.

TONO          And two more cocktails.

CYRIL         Certainly, my lord.

*CYRIL exits.*

NOEL          From the old cairn at the highest point of the island Plymouth is clearly visible. Devonport is sometimes visible.  Cape Trafalgar is clearly invisible.

TONO          What did Bobby Anstruther tell you about him?

J-BOY         The usual bosh. Colossal in every quarter.  Complacent in every bed.

NOEL          That doesn't surprise me.

23

TONO            He meant complaisant.

J-BOY            He meant completely complexly
companionable.

DICKIE            I should really be somewhere else but
I'm not there.  I'm here.

NOEL            Very sound.

DICKIE            I really do feel I ought to be there.

J-BOY            But you're not.

DICKIE            No, I've come here, with you.  To see I
don't know what.

J-BOY            You do know what.

DICKIE            I do know what.  But do I want?  Yes?

J-BOY            Yes.

DICKIE            Or no.  Or yes.

TONO            Edwina was in tiptop form at Dodo's on
Tuesday.  In silver lamé and a garnet rose, outshining even
Dodo, who forgot she'd invited the Grand Duke and wore
Bolshevik red from top to toe.

NOEL            No great distance upon Dodo.

DICKIE            *(coughs)* Gentlemen.   Please remember that the Imperial family is my family.   The late Tsarina was the youngest of my mother's sisters and a princess of Hesse.  Maria  Federovna,  the  late  Tsar's  paternal grandmother, was the sister of my paternal grandfather, and of my mother's paternal grandfather, who were of course brothers.

NOEL            Dickie, you clamber around your family tree like a topsailman in the rigging.  Landgraves ahoy!

DICKIE            Edwina and I are jolly madly in love.

NOEL            To be sure.   Until marriage puts an end to all that, you and J-Boy can jostle for Cyril's glad-eye.

DICKIE            Until marriage puts an end to all that.

*CYRIL enters with drinks.*

J-BOY            Commander Anstruther sends his fond
regards.

CYRIL            It's good of him to remember me, sir.

J-BOY            You gave him a weekend to remember.

CYRIL            I wouldn't have called it weak, sir.

25

*CYRIL exits.*

NOEL          I don't know what's come over the
working classes.  We're all of us far jauntier than we used
to be.

DICKIE          You're quite absurd, Noel.  We all work
nowadays. Every day on my Indian tour with the Prince
of Wales we had to entertain some tuppeny-ha'penny
maharajah. We returned with trunks of booty. Ivory
boxes, gold dishes, gold daggers.  I could stab 27 lovers and
leave a gold dagger in each.

*A beat*

J-BOY          *(to TONO)*  You'd have loved the little
Indians. They wriggle.

TONO          Noel and I will set sail on Tuesday.

DICKIE          What?  Noel,  I  want  you  at  the
wedding.

NOEL          Of course. What shall I give you to stab
into Edwina?

DICKIE          Oh. Ha ha. I think that part of the job's
up to me. Ha ha. She's a very special person, Noel. Very
special.

TONO            You make her sound like a white
elephant.

DICKIE          Really special. I'm a horribly lucky
fellow. Everything's going along all right. It's so thrilling.
When I think about Audrey. She was so tawdry. Whereas
Edwina, is so much keener.

NOEL            In her demeanour.

TONO            Like a hyena.

J-BOY           But obscener.

NOEL            On the other hand do you suppose
you'd feel serener to quarantine her? Or in the last resort
abruptly guillotine her.

DICKIE          No, she's really just the right person for
me.

TONO            We have a mysterious creature staying
here.

J-BOY           Oh Lord. Who?

TONO            She signed the register Arabelle Clifford
but Noel swears she's really someone called Agatha
Christie.

DICKIE          Who?

NOEL            A writer of useful guidebooks on how to
kill your wife and be caught.

DICKIE          I know who Agatha Christie is. Is she
here?

TONO            Noel recognised her from some
photographs.

NOEL            I never forget a celebrity. Evidently she
has no wish to be a celebrity, or not here and now. Why
not?

DICKIE          But that's incredible!

NOEL            Perhaps amusing to find out.

DICKIE          Noel —

NOEL            She's no fool. Fool-ish. There'll be some
crack in her armour.

DICKIE          Do stop talking, Noel. Sorry, but this is
important. Isn't it?

J-BOY           Providential.

DICKIE          Right. Because I've invented an
absolutely brilliant idea for a detective story.

TONO            Set on an island?

DICKIE          What? No.

NOEL            They were the footprints of a gigantic
mermaid.

DICKIE          Please. Nobody's ever thought of a
story as good as this. Don't look like that. It's true.

J-BOY           It is.

DICKIE          You see? Detective stories always have
to have someone who tells the story. Don't they? My idea,
which is truly brilliant, came during a Durbar at Indore
when the Prince had to smile and chat and nod and greet
this procession of rajahs. All he wanted to do was go off
and write another love-letter to Freddy. Freda. Freda. But
there he was, trapped. 'Wonderful to meet you.' 'Splendid
to meet you.' 'So interesting to meet you.' Into my head
popped this incredible idea. I don't have the time to write
it but she could, and I was just about to write her a letter
—

J-BOY           Tomorrow.

DICKIE          Tomorrow — and here she is! Don't you reckon that's quite extraordinarily extraordinary?

NOEL          Dickie, if you don't reveal your bloody idea quickly, I shall die of patience.

DICKIE          Right. Well. It's this. The chap who tells the story — the Dr Watson chap — he commits the murder.

TONO          How can he?

DICKIE          Because he's telling the story. He can put in what he wants, leave out what he wants. He leaves out it was he killed the vicar in the library in Chapter 1, and how he killed the frightful millionairess in Chapter 2. And in the last chapter he writes, 'Well, I hate to say it but the game's up. Monsieur —

J-BOY          Poirot

DICKIE          — Poirot turned to me this afternoon and said, "My friend, you are ze guilty one." It's never been done before. Ever. Ever. You read a book and you suspect all the people except the man who's telling the story. You have to trust him. You do trust him. But he is the murderer.

NOEL          Dickie, you astonish me.  More than that.  You bewilder me.  What led you to dream up such a treacherous idea?

*End of scene*

Scene 2

The same. Afternoon.

*CYRIL enters R carrying a tray of coffee cups, crosses and exits L. DICKIE enters C, glances around and is about to exit when CYRIL returns, carrying the empty tray.*

DICKIE          Where is Mrs Christie?

CYRIL           My lord?

DICKIE          Clifford. Mrs Clifford.

CYRIL           In the sun lounge, my lord, taking coffee.

DICKIE          Alone?

CYRIL           Alone at her table, my lord, but other residents are at their tables.

DICKIE          Well, is there another door out of the lounge?

CYRIL           Onto the terrace, my lord.

DICKIE          Damn.

CYRIL           May I take the lady a message?

32

*DICKIE shakes his head.*

When Mrs Clifford found this room empty yesterday, she played the piano. If it appeared to be empty today when she appeared, you could yourself appear. My Lord.

DICKIE          Yes. Yes. *(gestures dismissal)*

CYRIL          Thank you, my lord.

*CYRIL exits R.   DICKIE goes to stand out of sight C.  J-BOY enters with TONO.*

TONO          Have you ever been back to Mornington?

J-BOY          *(shakes his head)*  My mother ended up in Malvern.

TONO          My people still miss her.

J-BOY          She misses them.

TONO          You could come back.

*J-BOY sits on a table.*

Take the punt out.

*Pause*

J-BOY          What was the name of that appalling snooper?  His stinking moleskin jacket.

TONO          Garvin.  He's bedridden now.

J-BOY          Nothing trivial, I hope.

*DICKIE interrupts them.*

DICKIE          You must go.  You can't stay here.

J-BOY          Dickie.

DICKIE          Agatha Christie may want to play the piano.  Be so good.

J-BOY          I may want to play the piano.

DICKIE          You can't.

J-BOY          I could practise.  Tono used to play beautifully.

DICKIE          Not now.  *(an effort)*  Please.

TONO          We could go down and look at the sea.

J-BOY          I do enough of that from my ship.

TONO          You could explain what the different waves mean.

J-BOY          *(laughs)* You are an ass.

*They move off.*

I've missed that.

*TONO and J-BOY exit. DICKIE opens the piano lid, arranges the piano stool invitingly and returns to his hiding-place. AGATHA enters L. She closes the piano lid. Gazes bleakly around, turns to exit C and comes face to face with DICKIE.*

DICKIE          I do apologise. Mrs Clifford, I think. No, I won't pretend I think that.  In fact — Mrs Christie, I presume?  I am Lord Louis Mountbatten.

AGATHA          How do you do.

DICKIE          I really am delighted to have run into you. Really, truly. I was going to write to you tomorrow, believe it or not, care of your publisher. The Bodley Head. I've meant to write for weeks, months, but I've been at sea, and eight months in India with the Prince of Wales.

AGATHA          Your father must have been gratified when you followed him  into the Navy.

DICKIE          I never doubted where my future lay. He died last year. September 10<sup>th</sup>. He was able to meet my fiancée, the week before he died. And I met Sir Ernest Cassel, her grandfather, the week before he died. What is remarkable is that they both died in the same week. My father in bed, Sir Ernest at his desk, stretching out his hand to the bell-pull. I think of it as a special bond between us.

AGATHA          A man of some wealth, I believe.

DICKIE          Oh, enormous wealth. But do let's sit down. I feel as out of place as you would if you came up to me with suggestions for signal reform.

AGATHA          Why might I do that?

DICKIE          Exactly. It's not your field and this is not my field. Except in so far as all of us read, many of us read detective stories, and some of us — a precious few — write them. Or think up fiendishly ingenious plots. I'll come straight to the point. I have the most perfect plot there's ever been for a detective story. I haven't time to write it myself, but you can.

AGATHA          Lord Louis, that isn't how writing happens, you know.

DICKIE          But you always need a plot.

AGATHA          An author needs a plot, that's true.

DICKIE          So whether it comes from you or someone else doesn't matter. Now, Hercule Poirot has a Dr Watson fellow called Captain Hastings. Right? He tells the story. So far you've written stories where someone is killed and they turn up to investigate — well, Poirot's the one who investigates. Hastings is a dim foozle who gets hold of the wrong end of the stick and falls in love with redheads. But — this is the point — suppose he isn't such a numbskull. Suppose he committed the murder. And suppose he comes along with Monsieur Poirot because he can then dispose of any clues he left behind. As well as writing a record of what happens, concealing what really happened.

AGATHA          One moment. How could he write an acceptable story? His cast of mind would reveal the kind of person he is.

DICKIE          Not if he was a cunning, controlled, methodical murderer. It doesn't have to be Captain Hastings. Anybody you like but whoever tells the story — a woman if you want — she has to be the murderess. That's the brainwave. That's what your readers will never guess.

AGATHA          No, no, it wouldn't work at all. No, I couldn't possibly do that.

DICKIE          It would be easy. I mean, you'd have to think it out.  If there was a second murder you'd need to provide time for him to do it.  Or do it in a special way to provide an alibi.  A wire attached to a gun.  Or poison, of course, at a cocktail party with everyone moving around.  That's the detail.  But the shock is the revelation that the one person nobody will ever dream of suspecting is the killer.

AGATHA          Really, Lord Louis, it would be quite wrong, I assure you. There is a contract between the writer and the reader —

DICKIE          Break it.

AGATHA          And the contract is trust.

DICKIE          Betray it.

AGATHA          That would be treacherous.  Who could the reader trust in future!

DICKIE          No one.  Why should he trust anyone?

AGATHA          The writer —

DICKIE          Poppycock.  The detective story would never be the same again.  You could make it never the same  again.   By  being  the  murderer.  Of  course  it's

treacherous. Noel Coward said that. Why not? Your sales
would go through the roof.

AGATHA          Possibly. But, you see, I no longer think
of myself as a writer. I've written three or four books and
some stories —

DICKIE          I've read all of them.

AGATHA          — but I'm a little old-fashioned in that I
believe a woman who is a  wife  and  mother  should  be
primarily a wife and mother.  I have no more ideas for any
more detective books. And I don't intend to provide myself
with any.  So you must take your ingenious idea — thank
you  for,  for  considering  me  but  I  must  decline  the
compliment.

DICKIE          Think about it.  If you think about it I
know you'll find you're up to the task.

AGATHA          I can't have made myself clear.  It isn't
a task I wish to be up to.  One has to feel involved in even
the simplest story.  And I should not wish to feel involved
in this one — even if I had the inclination to write anything
ever again.  It takes a lot of time, you know.  Thinking and
writing, and thinking and rewriting. There are other things
in life that one should put first.  My husband is a keen
golfer.  If I can reduce my handicap I could be a partner
for him.  So if you'll excuse me — and thank you, I do

appreciate the honour, Lord Louis, it's most gratifying to learn that you have enjoyed my little efforts.

DICKIE          My mother will be disappointed. She's one of your greatest admirers.

AGATHA          I do always take a lie-down after luncheon.

*Awkwardly she exits C.*

DICKIE          Fuck. Double fuck.

*Stamps his foot. Controls himself. Takes out a pack of cards, sits and shuffles them. Continues shuffling them.    NOEL enters, glances at DICKIE, sits at the piano.*

                She disapproves of my idea.  On moral grounds.

NOEL            Idiotic.

DICKIE          She pretends she's going to stop writing. I want to play golf with my husband.

NOEL            Does she, indeed.

DICKIE          I'll take it to someone else.  And when it's published I'll send her a copy. 'To Mrs Christie, who did not appreciate what was too good for her.'

*NOEL sings a variation of his song 'Devon' from* London Calling.

NOEL     Oh! Hampshire men are hearty
      And Bolton men are bold,
      There's something coy in a Blackpool boy,
      And the Bedford lads have hearts of gold.
      But the chaps that live in Devon
      Are breezy, bright and gay.
      Singing a tra la la
      With a hey ho ha
      And a whack fol do
      And a nin nonny no
      And a down derry down, sing hey!
      Down derry down, sing hey!

DICKIE    *(putting cards away)* What's the matter with a woman like that? Wife and mother! When I become husband and father I shan't want Edwina trailing after me all the time.

NOEL     Is that likely?

DICKIE    I'd hate it. That's not my idea of love. Is it yours?

NOEL     I should loathe it.

DICKIE          Her husband will soon give her the boot if she tries that trick. Edwina will have her life and I'll have mine. You understand what I'm saying?

NOEL          Elaborate a little.

DICKIE          You can't spend every minute of every day together. It's unnatural.

NOEL          What about every minute of every night?

DICKIE          I'll tell you my idea of love. It's — it's not just — At Broadlands — Edwina's house, or it will be hers eventually — there's a really perfect lawn.

NOEL          A what?

DICKIE          It's so broad — Broadlands — it spreads right out to the —

NOEL          Ha-ha.

DICKIE          What?

NOEL          On the boundary. To keep the shuddering uddering cows at bay.

DICKIE          It goes right into the distance. You can build rows of pavilions on it. You could play fifty games of croquet. All the important rooms look onto it. It's there, whenever you go to a window. Wonderful to look at. But you don't want to go trailing over to the window all the time. That's how I see my love for Edwina.

NOEL          Tell me about her love for Dickie.

DICKIE          Well. That's it. She does. You can always tell, can't you. It's not just my connections. Sir Ernest, her grandfather, was awfully pally with the late king.    He went to Windsor so often they called him Windsor Cassel!

NOEL          Does her wealth embarrass you?

DICKIE          Why should it?

NOEL          It shouldn't for one instant. The miller's son who finds a purse of gold is well set, where a heart of gold will bring him nothing.

DICKIE          Except love.

*NOEL begins lightly to play the piano.*

          You've heard of love?

NOEL          Interminably. Written of it copiously. It's not, I assure you, a sound basement for the Leaning Tower of marriage.

43

DICKIE          What nonsense you talk.

NOEL            Ask anyone you know. Ask your
brother.

DICKIE          They're devoted.

NOEL            Because they're so reluctant to fuck. A
little now and then, for the sake of the title, but let's save
our energies for those we enjoy fucking. Will that be
Edwina?

DICKIE          I'm disappointed in you, Noel. You
climb into bed with any man you fancy and want
everybody to be the same as you.

NOEL            Heaven forfend.

DICKIE          It's an illness.

NOEL            Ah.

DICKIE          An affliction.

NOEL            And a sin?

DICKIE          I don't know about that.

*NOEL stops playing.*

NOEL          Do make it a sin.   One can generate
such moral fervour rounding on a sin.  Perhaps it is one of
those sins crying to heaven for vengeance.  I'm sure it
would cry a little if you asked it nicely.  I tell you this —
you are steaming into hell's whirlpool if you pretend that
one night with Edwina will sweep away your fancy for a
boy's bum or a boy's dickie.  Dickie.

DICKIE          You simply don't understand me at all.
I'd have thought you would but you don't want to, that's
what it is.

NOEL          If you want to hear my idea of love, it is
not just the longing to press oneself against some
enchanted skin.  Not just a prick song for bottom F.

DICKIE          I'm not listening to you.

NOEL          On the rare occasions when love deigns
to come our way, it is the frenzy to have some one person
in particular walk beside us: eat, drink, talk, listen, laugh,
sleep, fart alongside.  That is not what marriage is about,
after the first few months of careful rapture.  From rapture
to rupture unless, dear Dickie, gazing upon your perfect
lawn, you recognise that other grass is just as green and
fragrant.

DICKIE          You're so absolutely, stupidly wrong.
Really, you have got the most exaggerated opinion of your
knowledge of human nature.

*NOEL plays two impressive chords.*

I shall not betray Edwina.

*Another chord.*

And she will have no reason to betray me.

*A succession of imposing chords, ending when DICKIE slams shut the keyboard lid. NOEL just escape with his fingers. He stands.*

NOEL            If I struck you dead where you stand, would I be taken in chains to the Tower?  Behold the head of a truth-teller!  Your humble servant, m'lord.

*He bows, exits R.*

*(off)*  Cyril, a bottle of Pyrmont-water in my room.

CYRIL            *(off)* Yes, sir.

*DICKIE seethes with anger. He overturns the nearest table, sending an ashtray and a vase of flowers to the floor. CYRIL appears in the archway R.*

DICKIE            What are you staring at?  Get out!

*CYRIL remains where he is.*

Gutttersnipe!

*DICKIE walks off C. CYRIL rights the table, replaces the ashtray.*

CYRIL          Royal arsehole.

*He bends down to gather the flowers as J-BOY and TONO enter. TONO carries a length of seaweed. J-BOY is the first to see CYRIL.*

TONO          There was a young lady named Gloria.

J-BOY          Cyril?

TONO          Gloria.

CYRIL          The royal gentleman, sir. A little
accident.

TONO          Not royal, Cyril. Not any more.

CYRIL          No, my lord?

TONO          Once upon a time he was the Princess
Louisa of Battenberg.

CYRIL          Like the sponge cake, my lord?

TONO            Very like. Then came something called
the Great War. Hunnish Hohenzollerns and Horrible
Hapsburgs.

J-BOY           Svinish Saxe-Coburgs.

TONO            So the Boring Battenbergs had to
change their names and drop their royal handles.

CYRIL           Yes, I see, my lord. Batten-berg —
Mount-batten.

TONO            Bad enough having his father as First
Sea Lord.

CYRIL           Was that his father, my lord? The one
they sacked in 1914.

TONO            Couldn't risk him sending postcards to
the Kaiser.

CYRIL           Sounds a pretty rum do to me, my lord.

*Exits.*

J-BOY           Noel's very thick with Dickie.

TONO            Dickie likes someone to make him
laugh. Noel loves to snob- hob.

J-BOY          Do I?  It must look like that.  Perhaps I
have done.

*TONO drapes seaweed over J-BOY's head.*

               What about this young lady named
Gloria?

TONO           She was had by Sir Gerald du Maurier
               And then by six men,
               Sir Gerald again,
               And the band at the Waldorf-Astoria.

*They laugh.*
*CYRIL re-enters with cloth and pan to mop up.*

J-BOY          Lord Bungay and I were childhood
sweethearts, Cyril.

CYRIL          That's romantic, sir.

J-BOY          Where did you and the lovely Dennis
meet?

CYRIL          At the Battle of Jutland, sir.  Strictly
speaking, after the Battle of Jutland.  I was on the *Malaya*
and he was on the old *Tipperary*.  We met in Number 4
Hospital at Haslar.

*A beat*

J-BOY          I was on the *Malaya*. *(he removes the seaweed)*

CYRIL          Yes, sir. Under Captain Boyle, sir. Both our oppos bought it so we rub along with each other. Will that be all, sir?

*J-BOY silent.    TONO nods*
*CYRIL exits.*

J-BOY          Life goes on. Who'd have thought it. Eh? Did you think it, in the trenches? One day life will go on, and all this ghastliness will be as piffle before the wind.

TONO           Life goes on.

J-BOY          True. Hannah.

TONO           Hilda.

J-BOY          There was a young woman named Hilda
               Who claimed that no man ever filled her,
               Till  *(thinks)*

*AGATHA enters, agitated.*

AGATHA         Lord Bungay, I understand Mr Coward is in his room.  Would he object to being disturbed?

TONO            All hell would break loose.

AGATHA          But if it were important?

TONO            I could push a note under his door.

AGATHA          No, that wouldn't do. When? Does he
come out, when?

TONO            Is it some matter where I can be of
help?

AGATHA          I can wait. Yes. Yes, I can do that. *(to
J-BOY)*  Are prospects good for promotion in the Royal
Navy?

J-BOY           They are better in times of war. The
admirals lose a battle, get themselves tugged off and the
rest of us move up a peg.

AGATHA          Will Lord Louis find promotion comes
more easily?

J-BOY           *(after a pause)*   You must ask him. He
was wanting to speak to you.

AGATHA          He has spoken.

*Pause.*

J-BOY          And what a lovely speaking voice he has.  Strong but not guttural.

TONO          Not Germanically guttural.

J-BOY          Arrogant yet not quite intolerable.

TONO          Tuetonically arrogant.

AGATHA          Do you both dislike him?

J-BOY          Oh, not at all.  There are times when a certain fatigue is generated.  When for the umpteenth time we have to play rummy with his cards. They have the Mountbatten coat of arms in full colour on the back. The red and white lions for Hesse, the black stripes for Battenberg.

TONO          I hope there's a yellow border for Marzipan.

AGATHA          He came to me with the most disagreeable idea I've ever listened to. I know it's very modern and young to cock a snook at notions that have held good for generations and served us well. But expecting the public to want to hear — want to read — not just a confession, that would be different, but a plot to delude them.  That's what I understand it to be. We're to be taken into the mind of someone who is intent on hiding what she — or he — really thinks, by — no, not lying, not actually lying — not telling the full truth — in order to — The intention is to score off the public. Look, see how clever I am! Not even that. It's: Look but you're never going to know how clever I am! It's the mind of a person who wants to deceive the world.

*Pause.*

I recommend a visit to the farm on the mainland, just beyond where you left your cars, if you motored here. Joymans Farm. They do a really good Devonshire cream tea. Proper cream, just as it should be. If it's getting on for low tide, which it ought to be, that's what I'm going to treat myself to. On holiday I think one can. Did you notice how the flowers in the dining-room have revived?

*AGATHA exits.*

| | |
|---|---|
| TONO | She's mad. |
| J-BOY | Bit eccentric. |
| TONO | No. She's cuckoo. Or she's onto something |
| J-BOY | What? Dickie? |
| TONO | She had a hunter's glint in her eye. |

J-BOY          If she hated his story it won't have made him happy.

TONO          It's only a story. God in heaven! You'd think it was something important.

*DICKIE storms in, making for exit L.*

J-BOY          Dickie –

DICKIE          Don't speak to me!

*DICKIE exits.*

J-BOY          It *is* important.

TONO          We are in for a bumpy weekend. Why should it be important?

J-BOY          It may only be my sordid mind.

TONO          Well, it was your sordid mind got me through many a grim weekend.

*NOEL enters C.*

NOEL          I've just written something terribly clever, which I intend to read to you. I assume you have nothing more exciting to listen to.

TONO          You might be surprised.


*End of Act One*

ACT TWO

Scene 1

*The same.   Late evening.*
*AGATHA and NOEL sit on opposite sides of the stage. She*
*is not reading her book. He appears to be reading his.*

AGATHA          Mr Coward?

NOEL            Mrs Christie?

AGATHA          I'd like to talk to you about Lord Louis.

NOEL            He loves to talk about himself so why
shouldn't we.

AGATHA          You are his friend.  I'm afraid you may
not like everything I have to say.

NOEL            You rejected his idea for a story, and I
detest people trotting up to suggest ideas to me.  But really
it's better to say 'How kind' and forget all about it.

AGATHA          No, the matter's more serious than
that.

NOEL            What can he have done?

AGATHA          Not what he has done but what he might do. He's good-looking and well-connected. Too well-connected, even. But I came to know a number of young naval officers in the War, and my impression was that they are perceptive and efficient within their field, and of course very charming, but outside their field naïve to the point of idiocy.

NOEL          The sailors it has been my pleasure to meet were all voracious for mothering. At sea presumably they mother one another.

AGATHA          I daresay they do. He told me, with some pride, that you called his idea treacherous.

NOEL          The word occurred to me.

AGATHA          It also occurred to me, very powerfully. You would not remember the campaign waged at the beginning of the War by certain newspapers to have his father removed as First Sea Lord. It was argued, rightly perhaps, that it was foolish, dangerous even, to have a more or less German prince in command of the British fleet. I remember the general satisfaction when he was dismissed. Lord Louis must then have been a cadet at Osborne. They send them there so young. Thirteen or fourteen.

NOEL          Where can this conversation be taking us?

AGATHA          Please.  Bear with me.  It really is of the utmost importance I say what I have to say.

NOEL          My mother's advice to me was never to say anything I would not wish to see printed in the newspapers next morning.  For most occasions grotesquely stupid advice, but there are rare days when it could be heeded.

AGATHA          I am not talking lightly, Mr Coward. That is not what I do.  He is zealous for the reputation of one who was dear to him, who he sees as cruelly maligned and unjustly destroyed.  Where his father fell, he will rise. Time or chance or merit may take him to the top of the tree.  But what if it does not?  Or worse, what if he fears it might not?

NOEL          Mrs Christie —

AGATHA          Edwina Ashley is a very fine match for a young ambitious man.  But I used to know a young man when we lived in Torquay.  He married a girl of good family.  It was an advantageous match for him and he wanted that.  But he was not what you would call the marrying kind.

NOEL          I will not have you put your words into my mouth.

AGATHA          I would not call him the marrying kind. In less than a year he had lost his joie de vivre, and nothing pleased him, and one day he committed a crime. But he had already committed a crime in marrying her.

NOEL            There was a young man from Torquay
                Who invited an heiress for tea.
                Said he, 'I like crumpet,
                But dash it and lump it,
                This tart's too revolting for me.'

*Pause*

AGATHA          I invented the story I told you but it makes my point.

NOEL            If you hadn't confessed I would have walked straight out of the room. Though I might have suggested you take a stroll along the edge of the cliff in a high wind.

AGATHA          Mr Coward, please believe me. Someone may be about to betray himself. You know him. I do not. I only know what I feel. What is treachery? It is when I lie to you and convince you I speak the truth. Or if I lied to myself and convinced myself I spoke the truth. Or if Lord Louis lies to himself, never doubting that what he says is true, up to and after it is too late. It is the mind at war with itself. Secretly. I am afraid for him.

NOEL          Let me come to your point. If he is not
what you would call the marrying kind, the arms of his
wife, crisp with diamonds, will become as the clutch of an
armadillo. Sick with self-hatred, too greedy to divorce her,
raging against the country that destroyed his father, he
will slap on a false bald head and sell naval secrets to
Lenin.

AGATHA          So you see how vital it is for him not to
marry.

NOEL          May I call you Agatha?

AGATHA          Of course.

NOEL          You may call me Noel. Agatha, because
you write of treachery and crime, dear Agatha, can you
think of nothing else? We all treasure venomous snakes in
our bosom. All they ask is to be assured how much they
mean to us and they will not bite. Let sleeping snakes lie.

AGATHA          They do lie. When they say they are
sleeping, they lie. And what if they are not re-assured, and
never taken out and shown the world, but rage and hiss in
the snake-pit of the heart? They will spill out, Mr Coward.
And then they will bite.

NOEL          Oh dear, oh dear.

AGATHA            When I studied music in Paris,
Monsieur Debussy said to us, 'Why must dissonant chords
be resolved?'

*Sits at piano, plays dissonant chords, does not resolve them.*

                  Do you hear something waiting,
searching, clamouring to become . . .

*She resolves the chord.*

                  Unlike Monsieur Debussy I like to hear
dissonant chords resolved.  Not left to invade the world.

*Plays harshly dissonant chords.*

NOEL              What a deafening musical tragedy
you've composed from Lord Louis' innocent little theme
for a story.  It really won't do, you know, really it won't.

AGATHA            What did you say of Conan Doyle and
'Thor Bridge'?  Its lesson for us: Hold your tongue.

NOEL              Watch your tongue.  The crucial
difference seems to escape you.

AGATHA            Watch your tongue. It doesn't escape
me.

NOEL              Yet you propose to stop writing.

AGATHA          I have no immediate plans.

NOEL            You have Lord Louis' plot.

AGATHA          Yes. His plot.

NOEL            That's the second time in two minutes you have twisted my words to fit your lurid argument. My words are tough, wiry little creatures and if ill-treated will go for your heels like a gypsy's lurcher.

AGATHA          I have sometimes wondered why the few books I've written centre around murder. Other crimes but principally murder. People do like them. Sales of the *Strand Magazine* increase by one hundred thousand when they carry a story by Conan Doyle. They are neat puzzles. Dissonant chords resolved. Perhaps that's it, you see — detective stories are modern parables of good and evil. Instead of evil giving the game away by tripping us up with his cloven hoof, he disguises himself as a dumpy little husband, or a careful wife a little too fond of spraying the greenfly. A murder on the bridge, on the golf links, at the foot of a church tower, and for a moment the universe is in peril. Then comes Saint Sherlock or Saint Hercule or the saintly Father Brown and good prevails. But let us not be fooled. It has happened once, it can happen again. Another disguise, another betrayal in this slaughter-house of a world.

NOEL          Well, well, well, well. That's very
passionately spoken, brightly argued, yes. Ho hum. If
there is no murder without a motive, can a person write
about it without one?

AGATHA          To earn a few pounds?

NOEL          Would that reply satisfy Monsieur
Poirot?

AGATHA          I might say to him that if the goose
discovered why she laid the golden eggs, she might stop
laying them.

NOEL          Parbleu. Zut, alors. Per'aps ze goose
she will no longer be content wiv ze second-best, and she
start to lay ze diamond eggs.

AGATHA          I'm sure neither of us — I am putting
words into your mouth — neither of us would write a
sentence if the assumption was that what we make our
characters do we secretly want to do ourselves. I should
have wanted to kill my lover's wife, and my wife, and
several husbands. Does a motive have to exist for every
violent phrase? Every daydream of betrayal and deceit?

NOEL          Why not?

AGATHA          Don't you think Lord Louis has the
motive for deceiving those who trust him? Demagogues

broke his father. How did his fellow cadets treat him in his years at Osborne, bearing a German princely name in a war against German princes? If Conan Doyle reveals himself in the story he wrote, as you suggested, hasn't Lord Louis revealed himself in the story he dare not write?

NOEL　　　　　It's such a pity you don't want to use his story. You'd lull our suspicions with such a graceful touch. You tried to distract my attention — no, I'll admit it, you did pull your woolly knitting right over my eyes with your talk of good and evil and golden eggs. You have a gift for sending us up a gum tree. Your books are avenues of gum trees, up which you send us. I employ a more direct route. Though I'm not against using a little subterfuge at the beginning.

AGATHA　　　　I'll remember to be on my guard.

NOEL　　　　　When are you ever off it? There's just one problem. You've come to the wrong Dutch uncle. Lord Louis and I have had what lovers would call a tiff. I certainly can't go and tell him to give up the Navy, breach his promise to Edwina and depart to grow tea in Ceylon. You see how melodramatic your fears sound, and even though I have spent years of my life reading Anthony Hope and Marion Crawford and William le Queux and authors I daresay you've never heard of. Stanley J. Weyman. Rhoda Broughton . . .

AGATHA     I assure you I am familiar with them all.

NOEL       Stanley J. Weyman?

AGATHA     *Under the Red Robe.*

NOEL       *The Castle Inn?*

AGATHA     Of course.

NOEL       *The Abbess of Vlaye?*

AGATHA     That was a little silly.

NOEL       But thrilling. What others?

AGATHA     *Starvecrow Farm.*

NOEL       Ah, poor little what's-her-name?

AGATHA     Jenny. The *Story of Frances Cludde.*

NOEL       What others?

*Pause*

AGATHA     *Lady Arabelle's Smile.*

NOEL       What is Lady Arabelle's story?

*Pause*

AGATHA          Arabelle Clifford's marriage is unhappy.
I congratulate you.

NOEL            A little subterfuge but otherwise direct.

AGATHA          I had forgotten.

NOEL            Remind me.

AGATHA          There's no need.

NOEL            At first she can't believe her husband
has a mistress. But then she finds a letter and that is the
end of him. No — wait.

AGATHA          I must pack.

NOEL            In the middle of the night?

AGATHA          I must leave.

NOEL            I presume Mr Christie is still alive?
Splendid.   It is no business of mine why you should toy
with the satisfactions of killing him.

AGATHA          You can't think that.

NOEL            I absolutely do.

AGATHA          I love my husband very much.

NOEL            Of course you love him.  If you did not
you wouldn't have come out in a muck sweat at the idea of
writing a story from the point of view of a murderer.

AGATHA          Your words are extremely hurtful.

NOEL            Don't be distracted by that.  If you
don't want to think of killing somebody, you won't want to
think of killing anybody.  If all you write about is killing,
you'll want to stop writing entirely. That would be a pity
because you do it remarkably well.  Why you should do it
at all is something else.  Fashionable psychology would say
it's an unconscious wish to kill your father.

AGATHA          My father died when I was eleven. I
loved him very much.

NOEL            Fashionable psychologists would take
note of that.  Perhaps a soon-to-be-fashionable playwright
might suggest a connection between — No. I am
impertinent.  I cannot abide people prying into my life and
unmistakably you feel the same. I am not mistaken?

AGATHA          I do not care to parade myself before all
and sundry.

NOEL            Precisely.  And whether we parade
ourselves night and day or watch cunningly from behind a

screen, we can retain our privacy if we are watchful. But if we are to watch our tongues, we must know what they are tempted to say. It is intolerable when people we care for betray our devotion. I am not surprised you should absent yourself from domesticity awhile. But in this harsh world draw thy breath and tell another story. We are fortunate, you and I. We can tuck our feelings into a typewriter and leave them there to play out their wicked pranks.

AGATHA          One can spend too much time at the typewriter.

NOEL          Do you find that? It's my experience that once I start tap-tapping away I hardly know how to stop. Well, of course one stops when one has completed the job in hand. But there's always the next hand, so on it goes.

AGATHA          And a marriage calls for time to be spent on it. I could, of course, if I chose to do so, write another story. I prefer not to.

NOEL          I am powerless before your preferences. Never risk one's own happiness to make another happy. Lord Louis would  have felt he was contributing to English literature, which, God knows, no member of his family has done since Henry VIII scribbled down the lyrics for 'Greensleeves'. But I suspect his story can't be written. Why would a murderer want to describe his crime? It's Macbeth keeping a diary. 'Walked back over the heath, met three old ladies cooking a stew.' It wouldn't work at all.

AGATHA        Oh, no. One could have the murderer writing an account of this sensational event in a small community. Wanting to see how different people respond He could be the village doctor, perhaps. Village doctors know everybody. The retired colonel tells him why he thinks So-and-so was murdered. Had he a secret? 'Yes, yes, I remember hearing —' and so forth. The snowball of rumour, rolling in the wrong direction. It could be done very easily.

*Pause*

          But my writing would not satisfy him. Putting 'Arabelle Clifford' in the hotel, register, at random, was a signpost to anyone with eyes to see it. 'Thor Bridge' may be a signpost, I agree. If you do not care to see where the sign in Lord Louis' story points to, then I have been wasting my breath.

NOEL        You deduce that if he disappoints Edwina, not being the marrying kind, he might well — or rather, not well but wickedly . . . No, I can't bring myself to finish the sentence.

AGATHA        I'm not a fortune teller, Mr Coward.

NOEL          I can't imagine what I could say to him! What an admission. I've never heard myself confess such a thing. Dickie, the safety of the country depends on your leaving the Navy.

AGATHA          I can't do better than repeat his words to me. 'Think about it and I know you'll find yourself up to the task.'

NOEL          His mother's voice to a T. What did you reply?

AGATHA          I said it wasn't a task I wanted to be up to. But my decision is a personal matter, of small consequence to the world at large.

NOEL          I shall have to convince myself your suspicions have some modicum of plausibility. And even then he's dead set on marrying Edwina.

AGATHA          She will not make him happy.

NOEL          Oh, this mania for pursuing happiness through fantasies of mutual desire! Very well. Set me an impossible task. What do I care!

AGATHA          I knew I could depend on you, Mr Coward.

NOEL          Everyone    depends    on    me.    It's
insufferable.   Where  shall  I  find  someone  I  can  tell  my
troubles to?

AGATHA        Is that what you would like?

NOEL          I   should   detest   it.   Good   night,   Mrs
Christie.

AGATHA        Mr Coward.

*As they are walking off . . .*

*End of scene*

Scene 2

The same.   The following morning.

*J-BOY is cautiously playing a child's piano piece, perhaps Beethoven's Minuet in G.*

*DICKIE enters.*

DICKIE          A boat leaves in 45 minutes.   We'll take it.

*J-BOY continues to play.*

                I hate people playing the piano when I'm talking.

J-BOY          It might be just as true to say I hate people talking when I'm playing. As I used to tell my younger sister: I got first to the tit.

*But he has finished the piece.*

DICKIE          You're behaving very oddly.   You have all weekend.   We'll find lunch on the way.

J-BOY          I haven't walked round the island yet.

DICKIE          It's only an island, for God's sake.   One side's the same as the other.

J-BOY           Cyril says there'll be venison for lunch.

DICKIE         They won't know how to cook it. It has to be served on double plates to retain the heat. You're lucky not to be eating it. You'd have had the bellyache all afternoon.

J-BOY            Even so —

DICKIE         You better get a move on. I've packed...

*CYRIL enters.*

CYRIL           Mr Coward's compliments, my Lord. He wonders if you will join him in a cup of coffee, if it's not too tight a fit.

DICKIE         What?

CYRIL           *(reads from a scrap of paper)* 'Join me in a cup of coffee, if it is not too tight a fit.' My Lord.

DICKIE         No. We're leaving.

J-BOY            Dickie —

DICKIE         He'll only play the piano at us and I won't have that.

*NOEL bounds in, sporting a white cloth over his arm and carrying a tray with coffee and biscuits.*

NOEL             Good morning, Sir. Coffee? Certainly, Sir. This table looks convenient; very convenient and circular. *(puts tray on table)*

DICKIE           Noel —

NOEL             And for the young gentleman coffee on the terrace? Very suitable indeed, sir; very alfresco and panoramic.

DICKIE           What are you playing at?

NOEL             I'm so much better at waiting on people than waiting for them. A Nice biscuit? A not-so-Nice biscuit? The other young gentleman was making enquiries about your whereabouts, Sir. Yes, a very taking young gentleman, Sir; very affable and taking indeed, Sir.

DICKIE           J-Boy —

J-BOY            We leave in 45 minutes. I know.

NOEL             On the terrace, Sir. Immersed in the antirrhinums.

*J-BOY exits.*

Thank you, Cyril.

CYRIL                Thank you, Sir.

*CYRIL exits*

DICKIE               Now what the devil are you doing?

*NOEL holds out his hand.*
*DICKIE grasps it enthusiastically.*

Noel, I was a frightful boor.

NOEL                 I flew right off my handle.

DICKIE               But flew back on your broomstick.

*A beat*

NOEL                 Absolutely.

DICKIE               I've been on edge for so long. I live on a
short fuse and it's shorter than ever it used to be.

NOEL                 I sympathise. You think I don't but I
do. So you're leaving?

DICKIE               I don't know. I don't know what I'm
doing. I don't. One minute I'm up, the next I'm down. If
it's love, it's horrible.

75

NOEL          Agatha's in love.  So much so that she's run away from her husband in order to decide whether to run back to him.

DICKIE        Is she going to?

NOEL          Until the next time. I told her your idea for a story couldn't possibly work, so at once she started making it work.  The family doctor, the gossiping colonel.

DICKIE        Oh, how clever you are!  Pretending you — ?  Ha!

NOEL          Whether she writes it down depends on whether she's going to live her life and not someone else's. That's the fetish that wrecks our threescore years and ten. Daughters living their mother's lives, sons living their father's lives, young wives deluded by old wives' tales of what a wife should be.

DICKIE        You're working round to something.

NOEL          It does sound terribly like it.  Is there a Mount Batten, up which ramblers in lederhosen ramble?

DICKIE        There is a castle, near Marburg.  Why?

NOEL          Have you ever been there?

DICKIE          Of course.  Occasionally.  Why are you
interested?

NOEL            I'm casting around for a topic of
conversation.  We could talk about me.  My career.  My
future.  My past.  I wish you'd seen me in *Peter Pan*.

DICKIE          Did you play Peter?

NOEL            That role would have required surgery
too extreme even for my ambition. I played Slightly, so
named because his pyjamas were marked 'Slightly Soiled'.
It was not much on which to build a character but I
slightly upstaged everyone I worked with.

DICKIE          I love Peter Pan. When he kills Captain
Hook.

NOEL            Ah, when.

DICKIE          On the ship.

NOEL            It's divine. That was in 1914. I was
fourteen.

*A beat*

DICKIE          I was fourteen.

NOEL          Each of us stepping forth to create our futures. Were you flogged at the mizzen-mast when slow at your semaphore?

DICKIE          I was brilliant at semaphore.

*He waves his arms through fourteen positions.*

NOEL          Astounding.

DICKIE          Know what I just said?

NOEL          It's on the tip of my flag.

DICKIE          God save the King.

*He repeats the last four positions: the K, I, N and G.*

          It's such a perfect sight when a ship's dressed overall and the ratings are drawn up in lines along the deck. Really, there's nothing grander in the whole world. I wish I wasn't going. No, no, I have to get back. I have to get back. *(sits)* What am I going to do?

NOEL          Rise to the top, as I shall rise. Though it will be easier for me. In the theatre there's room for everyone at the top. There are so many tops, glittering away up there, though I intend to sit on most of them. In the Navy only one man at a time gets to be top sea-dog.

DICKIE          I'll get there. Don't you fret about that.
I promised my father. I told him I will, so I will.

NOEL          Fine words.

DICKIE          Fine deeds too. My father loved this
country. He wasn't born here but this became his home.
The Royal Navy was his life. And he was hounded out.
You know about that. My mother was attacked. My
brother was attacked. At Osborne I was called a German
spy. Because of my name, my name only. But I'll tell you
one thing for nothing. When I get there they won't boot *me*
out. Let them try!

NOEL          In order to become — what is it? — First
Sea Lord, don't you have to sail off and win the occasional
battle? Which I'm sure you'd do most gallantly, standing
astride your dreadnought. But people keep telling me
there'll be no more war. Suppose they are actually right?

DICKIE          I shall do everything needful to redeem
my father. I don't think you appreciate how important
this is. Unless I can stand where he stood, do what he did
— and was prevented from doing! — If I can't one day
change the two stripes here *(gestures at his lower sleeve)* for
the broad stripe and four . . . crossed batons up here *(the
shoulders)* . . . gold oak-leaf sword-belt, there's no point my
going back to my ship now or ever. Which I have to do.

NOEL          You'll forgive my ignorance, but surely your father committed no crime?

DICKIE          Certainly he didn't! What do you mean?

NOEL          So redeeming him isn't what's required.

DICKIE          Isn't it? Redeeming? Doesn't it mean that? I have to undo what was done. Or do what was undone. I know what I have to do. So you see why I have to marry Edwina.

NOEL          Ah.

DICKIE          I know you dislike her.

NOEL          She's exquisite.

DICKIE          Don't fob me off. Why can't you say what you think?

NOEL          She's sophisticated, rather chilly, deceptively fragile, and likes to be thought fast but isn't.

DICKIE          That's true. Yes, that's her.

NOEL          What is she worth?

DICKIE          You see I'm not embarrassed by that question. There is envy of her wealth. It's not openly said but I know chaps are thinking of that.  We expect it to be about £50,000 a year

NOEL              What is J-Boy worth?

DICKIE              I've no idea. He'll earn the same as I do. Three hundred. But that's not it. She loves me.  She wants us to marry. I can't make her a Princess because I'm not allowed to call myself a Prince any more.  Since the King... quite understandably, took our German titles away.  But I can make her royal, and that's something when you think her grandfather started off as a money-changer in Cologne. All credit to him. Clever fellow. Good sort too. The late King invited him to Windsor so often he was known as Windsor Cassel. *(laughs)*  Well, she'll enjoy all that side of it, won't she.  She's bound to.  Look.  In time of war, yes, battles can be won, that's the way to do it.  Peacetime you have to find other ways of making a splash.

NOEL              Other than sinking a ship.

DICKIE              I'm serious.  I've worked it out. Carefully.  Very carefully indeed.  Edwina and I will make this name for ourselves.  Not just by entertaining, though we'll do plenty of that.  At Broadlands.  Brook House. Sir Ernest had four or five places.  Moulton Paddocks. Branksome. There'll be Classiebawn one day.

NOEL              Dickie, I won't ask if you've been to bed with a woman because you will tell me if you had.  But

81

I daresay the more connections one has had of a similar nature the merrier the wedding night.

*DICKIE nods.*

Perhaps I shall write a bright sketch about a wedding night. The pert chambermaid turning down the sheets. Loosening the curtains around the four-poster. In comes the mother of the bride, fussing about. And the grandmother of the bride. And Aunt Mabel. All these women twittering. And then — the newly-weds. He bold and dashing. She shy, nervous, not quite sure of herself. But sure of him. She longs for him. And then the inner curtains . . . and the outer curtains . . . close . . .

DICKIE          Noel, I can do what's necessary there, I'm sure. I mean, it's straightforward, isn't it. How can you go wrong? What bothers me is that it's not going to be just for the one night. She'll want more than that. They do, don't they. I won't always be at sea.

NOEL          However she reviews the opening night she'll have planned on a long run.

DICKIE          She will. She will. The thing is it's such an ideal match. My father approved of her. Of course she was on her best behaviour that day. She can be a bit pernickety.

NOEL            I wonder if my father would approve of
Tono?

DICKIE            I hardly think so.  Well, I don't know.

NOEL            Whether he does or not is of no
consequence.  My father is a sweet old soul, terribly proud
of his grown-up Noely, but I have to take on trust the
notion that any man does anything of which his son can be
proud.

DICKIE            My father —

NOEL            It's an achievement of a sort to have
stayed for thirty years married to my mother without at
some time boiling her down into glue.

DICKIE            You can't say things like that!

NOEL            Don't misunderstand me.  I love them
dearly, and dearly have I paid for it.  Because their battles
are not our battles, and our defeats are not their victories.

DICKIE            My father's battles are my battles.

NOEL            No!  Oh, Dickie, we haven't much time.
Another fifty years and we shall both be tucked up in our
coffins, no morning call, please, no last trump.  No darkness
because we shall not be here to tell darkness from light.

Nothing. Perhaps applause. And then the everlasting curtain.

DICKIE          Are you afraid of death?

NOEL          I shall be, if I haven't lived. *Life* is the awfully big adventure. Daddies disappoint, and mummies couldn't be more boring if they took lessons from the Queen of Holland. Don't tell me she is your Aunt Wilhelmina.

DICKIE          No. My Great-uncle Leopold married Hélène, the sister of Queen Emma, who was —

NOEL          To hell with all that frigging in the rigging. This is the age of the dreadnought. Dread nought. Least of all a father's commands to be what he was not — or worse still, be what he was.

DICKIE          You'd like to be helpful, I'm sure. But it isn't just what I swore to my father I'd do, last year at his deathbed. It's what I swore to myself I'd do, when I was fourteen, when my father had been booted out and the other cadets were chalking Dirty Bosche over my bed-head. That's when I swore I'd one day be what they'll never be. I'll make that happen, Noel. I'll make that happen.

*CYRIL enters.*

CYRIL          My Lord —

NOEL           Go away.

CYRIL          Yes, Sir.

NOEL           Though not too far away.

CYRIL          No, Sir.

*CYRIL exits.*

DICKIE         And Edwina will be at my side.

NOEL           What I really want at this moment is to
stretch my fingers on that piano but your proximity makes
me nervous.

DICKIE         Oh, Noel, I'm sorry, I'm sorry. Are they
all right?

NOEL           Not a mark.

DICKIE         I do that, you know. I suddenly snap
and do what some people object to and then they want to
hate me.   But they can't keep it up because I'm too
charming. I charm you. I charm everyone. I ought to still
be a Prince.

NOEL                So: Edwina.  Oedipus Rex woke up one
morning with the secret of the universe on his lips.

DICKIE              Is this true?

NOEL                It was certainly not the secret of the
universe. What he fondly thought was the secret came to
him in this artless verse. Hogamus higamus, man is
polygamous.  Higamus hogamus, woman monogamous.

*Laughter from DICKIE.*

                    For thousands of years, from Mr Rex all
the way down to Mrs Christie, this was held to be the secret
of well-being.  Mrs Christie goes further.  Hogamus
hogamus, all stay monogamous.  She's having difficulty
picking her way across that particular wasteland.

DICKIE              That's right.  She is.

NOEL                The secret of well-being is infinitely less
exhausting. Sex may seem an enthralling occupation but it
is, in truth, a quite pestiferous nuisance. Vital to our
health, like mother's cottage pie. But not to be gobbled
down daily. Or nightly. Even weekly.

DICKIE              How do you mean?

NOEL                If someone comes along and looks tasty,
how delicious.

86

DICKIE          You and Tono?

*A dismissive gesture from NOEL.*

                That's it, you see. I don't like doing it. I
don't mind seeing it. I don't want to do it.

NOEL            Edwina will. There is no doubt there.
How will you cope with her perfectly everyday demands?
You can charm the hind-leg off a donkey but you can't
make use of that in bed. So? You do what you can. Don't
let her expectations unnerve you. A man cannot give more
than he has to give. And you provide her with absolute
buckets-full of something else. One day, when you
command your own ship, how will you stop your crew
deserting?

DICKIE          What? I can't flog them at the yard-
arm.

NOEL            And that might not work on HMS
Edwina.

DICKIE          Oh, I see. Make them want to stay.
Make her want to stay.

NOEL            Enchant her in every waking hour. I
mean enchant. Dazzle her with your relatives, order your
sailors to cheer whenever she steps aboard.

DICKIE          She is fascinated by me.

NOEL            When that passes — and it will, but
don't grieve — keep the sailors cheering. Let her buy you
a yacht. Buy you a castle. You are no longer a Prince and
she is no Cinderella, but if you live your marriage as a fairy
story you could keep us all enchanted.

DICKIE          Do you think so?

NOEL            *(calls)* Cyril!

DICKIE          You make it sound so easy.

*CYRIL enters.*

NOEL            A box of cigarettes.

CYRIL           Yes, sir.

*CYRIL exits.*

DICKIE          Why shouldn't the sailors cheer her?

NOEL            Absolutely.

DICKIE          She'll love that.

NOEL            Is it true that Nelson put his telescope
to his blind eye so as not to observe what he didn't want to
see?

DICKIE          So they say.

NOEL            Always wise to keep a blind eye handy.
I can't think Agatha's man will stop running after bits of
fluff.

DICKIE          I think I understand what you're
driving at. Am I right?

NOEL            Human nature is what it is. And in this
respect there are women who can be quite as human as
men.

DICKIE          You're very wise, you know that, don't
you. Of course you do. Oh, God, you're going to be my
father now.

NOEL            At the risk of disappointing you cruelly,
I may never put you across my knee to spank your botty.

DICKIE          You are an ass!

*J-BOY enters.*

J-BOY           I'm packed and ready.

DICKIE          Oh, we don't have to go yet.

J-BOY           I'm ready to go.

DICKIE          We don't need to.

J-BOY           Then I will.

DICKIE          Very well. You'll have to become more flexible if you want to rise in the service.

J-BOY           Is that what I'll need?

DICKIE          You're coming to the wedding?

NOEL            Delighted.

*AGATHA enters, in travelling clothes.*

DICKIE          Ah, the lady who has the good sense to change her mind.

NOEL            Be off with you.

DICKIE          Don't call the murderer 'Dickie'. Or yes! You can! Tricky Dickie! Ha-ha! Goodbye, Noel. I'll give your love to Edwina.

NOEL            And kisses.

DICKIE          O-oh? Have you settled up?

J-BOY           All done.

DICKIE          Good man. Goodbye. Goodbye.

AGATHA          Goodbye.

*DICKIE and J-BOY exit.*

NOEL            Have I failed or have I succeeded? Both. One cannot do better than that. He will marry Edwina, but when the scales fall from his eyes — and from her eyes — he won't let it agitate him.

AGATHA          Poor young girl.

NOEL            There are worse fates than being married to a man who has ceased to love one.

AGATHA          Indeed?

*NOEL briefly non-plussed.*

                I shall follow his career with close attention.

*She turns to go.*

NOEL            I have disappointed you.

AGATHA          We must wait to see. If Lord Louis
comes to believe that nothing he does can ever be faulted,
he may be able to bully his way to where he thinks he
ought to be. It is still a matter, isn't it, of how he sees
himself.

NOEL          He is profoundly in love with Lord
Louis.

AGATHA          Profoundly is not quite right.
Desperately. Does that sound curious to you? I think there
are many people who cling, so to speak, desperately to
themselves. Like a drowning man who won't bring himself
to trust anything else. Anyone else. Of course we should
love ourselves. The importance of that has never been
sufficiently stressed. Love thy neighbour, yes, but I would
put the injunction the other way round. Love thy self as
thou loveth thy neighbour. I wonder if you detect the
difference? Not that we should become our neighbour's
keeper. There I am in agreement with Cain. The answer to
'Am I my brother's keeper?' must be No. Otherwise we
slide into sentimentality and worse.

NOEL          Worse?

AGATHA          Fatuous self-sacrifice.

NOEL          Yes.

AGATHA          Not that I am suggesting we should become our brother's murderer. And to save you suspecting another family melodrama —

NOEL          — you have no actual brother. What an education this weekend has proved to be! Perhaps no more troubled heroines with red hair?

AGATHA          *(after thought)* So far only two.

NOEL          Don't forget the acrobatic redhead on the golf links.

AGATHA          Will you never allow your heroes to play the piano?

NOEL          Frequently. But they will never sigh for the love of a laddy.

*CYRIL enters, bringing NOEL a box of cigarettes.*

          Thank you. Look Mrs Clifford in the face. What do you see there? Go on.

CYRIL          Mrs Clifford's — Your face, ma'am.

NOEL          And behind the face? *(as Cyril moves to look behind her)* Within it, Cyril. Within those steady eyes, that firm mouth and resolute chin?

CYRIL          I don't understand, sir.

NOEL          The best possible answer. *(to AGATHA)* Remain a sphinx and the world will beat a path to your bookstall.

AGATHA          You may stop looking at me now, Cyril.

CYRIL          Thank you, ma'am. The porter has brought the luggage downstairs.

*She nods. CYRIL exits.*
*NOEL advances to shake hands.*

NOEL          Perhaps our paths will cross again. You must let me know if ever the Prince of Wales approaches you with the idea for some sordid romance.

*AGATHA crosses to the piano, plays a single note.*

AGATHA          Nonetheless, fidelity is not to be ridiculed. Fidelity to another person, not simply to oneself.

NOEL          Do you suppose I think otherwise?

*Pause*

AGATHA          I did suppose it. Well. I shall be at Sunningdale by four o'clock.

94

NOEL                Infidelity has its place. Unless we are unfaithful to ourselves, when it adds up terribly quickly to a crime.

AGATHA            There I must disagree with you again. Unfaithfulness to oneself, as you call it — treachery — can malform us slowly. We may not even observe how we are changing. But I think most of us would notice how it begins.

*She mouths goodbye, and exits.*
*NOEL sits at the piano, plays idly.*
*After a few moments TONO appears in the archway R.*

NOEL                We shall be back to our two bouncing selves tonight.

*TONO glances at his watch.*

                    Their ferry is kicking at the pricks. I believe it is something quite allowed in oriental boxing.

*TONO comes to stand behind NOEL, rests a hand briefly on his shoulder.*

TONO              Noel, my dear, I'm leaving with J-Boy.

NOEL              Nonsense.

TONO              I can hardly believe it myself.

NOEL            What are you talking about? What do
you mean?

*TONO moves away.  NOEL stops playing.*

                Come here.

TONO            I'm perfectly at ease over here.

NOEL            If you think that by standing there I
shan't raise my voice to you, I shall. *(does so)* I shall raise
Cain, the roof, and lumps on your skull by throwing
anything to hand. *(picks up ashtray)*

*TONO moves towards him.*

                What has been going on under my nose
here, behind my back?

TONO            Difficult to manage both at once.

NOEL            Serpents rise to the challenge.

TONO            J-Boy and I were too ignorant to love
each other when we were boys. We've never been alone
together since, till this weekend.  And now we're in love.

NOEL            Stop drivelling like a *Peg's Paper*
parlour-maid.

TONO            I'm telling you the truth.

NOEL            The truth is you slunk down here to
enjoy an assignation with that toad.

TONO            You know that's absurd.

NOEL            Don't lie to me! I'm surrounded by liars
and cheats who screech at me: Dance! Sing! Astonish me!
Shock me! And what do I get in return?

TONO            Exactly what you want. Champagne
and cottage pie.

NOEL            I get you — who betray me at the first
chance you have to burrow into the carcase of your calf-
love. You leave me alone with nothing to do but pour oil
on minor royalty. I've seen the two of you slinking off
together. Little glances, secret whispers, strolling on the
seashore like Gert and Mabel. It's contemptible. Stop
fidgeting!

TONO            Noel —

NOEL            Don't 'Noel' me! You came down here
with malice aforethought to abandon me. *(TONO shakes
his head)* That's what last Wednesday was about.

TONO            Wednesday?

NOEL            Don't feign ignorance. It doesn't suit you.

TONO            I was dog-tired.

NOEL            I knew then something was going on in your wretched little head. You don't mean this. You can't mean it. When I first caught sight of you in that ridiculous orange bar in Curzon Street I thought, with a kind of awe-struck wonder: I've found it! This truly happens! It's not just a climax for Act Two and a rhyme for 'shove'. It isn't a half-hour in bed and thank you kindly. It's you and me, Tono. Sharing lives.

TONO            So what is it, which isn't just a rhyme for 'shove' and 'stars above'? Is it so very hard to pronounce?

NOEL            I was insane enough to imagine you felt the same. What blind folly! What stinking madness!

TONO            Do listen, Noel. Surely you can at a moment like this.

NOEL            What for, when I know with boring certainty everything you will say! I'm too much for you. I'm too little for you. God, how sordid. I stifle you. I neglect you. I only love you because your great-great-grandma was handed a title for sleeping with Charles the Second.

TONO            George the Second.

NOEL            I don't care if she opened her cuneiform
to Rameses the Second!

TONO            Do we love each other?  You see? You
hate loving. You hate yourself for loving. You don't look
for it. When it comes, you don't want it. When you can't
deny it's there, it makes you happy. But you hate being
made happy that way. I've watched you.

NOEL            Spied on me.

TONO            Noel.

NOEL            You shit.  You turd.

TONO            Do you want us to end like this?

NOEL            I believe in calling a turd a turd.

TONO            I am glad to say I have never seen a
turd.

NOEL/TONO       It is obvious that our social spheres
have been widely different!

*NOEL doubles up with slightly hysterical laughter.*

NOEL          Can you seriously run off with J-Boy when you could stay with me? What do you want me to do? Warm your slippers and wash your smalls? Tono.

TONO          Might that have been a joke? You're such a joker. Witty. Really it's exhilarating being in your company. But living with you... whoever you are... Soon enough somebody will find the courage to put on that play of yours, and before you hang up your typewriter you'll have written I don't know how many, marvellously clever and entertaining. And songs, scores more of them. But only once in every twenty years will you tell us anything you really feel.

NOEL          What nonsense are you burbling about?

TONO          And Dickie will get what he's after. More than he dreams possible, maybe. It'll be an achievement for the grandson of an illegitimate princeling. But there's nothing else to him, you must see that. Already his only hobby is tracing all the different ways he thinks he is descended from Charlemagne. The poor mutt. And Mrs Christie. There hasn't been a credible emotion in anything she's written. Not one convincing hint of a passion that alters a character as it lives. You can hide yourself if you want to. No law orders you to tell what you feel about living in this world. Go on being what you look like being. But I don't want to be a partner to that.

NOEL          Don't leave me. I'm unhappy. Can't
you believe that?

*TONO nods.*

              But you'll apply no remedy? Though it
lies within your power.

TONO          I think love has to be honest. J and I
may not be able to manage that.

NOEL          Look at me.

TONO          We may have to call it a day and go
back to picking up what comes rolling by.

NOEL          *(quiet)* Tony.

TONO          Things end. What good comes from
pretending they don't? That'd be betraying yourself,
again.

*A beat*

NOEL          I'd be terribly grateful if you'd now just
turn and walk smartly away. You were always
marvellously smart. Yes — say goodbye.

TONO          Goodbye, Noel.

*TONO exits R.*
*NOEL crashes a mighty dissonant chord.*

NOEL              Fuck, fuck, fuck!

*He plays the chord again, less mightily, and begins to resolve it through other chords until he is picking out 'Yes, We Have No Bananas'.*
*He rises from the piano, rings the bell.*
*Cyril enters at once with a cocktail on a tray.*

                  You stand not upon the order of your coming, but come at once.

CYRIL             Thank you, Sir.

*The cocktail is blue.*

NOEL              What are you proffering me?

CYRIL             Something new, Sir.

NOEL              Very nautical.

*CYRIL places bowls of nuts on the tables.*
*NOEL sits.*

                  How are the nuts this morning?

CYRIL             They seem a little perkier, Sir.

NOEL            And Dennis, who we never see?

CYRIL           He has his friends, Sir, and I have mine.

*He places a bowl of nuts on NOEL's table.*
*NOEL rests a hand on his.*

            Sir?

*NOEL moues a kiss. CYRIL glances around, kisses NOEL.*

            Will there be anything else, sir?


*End of play*